Sleep Well

Why You Need to Rest

by Kathy Feeney

Consultant:
Glenn Roldan, RPSGT
Clinical Director
California Center for Sleep Disorders
Sleep Consultant and Educator

Bridgestone Books
an imprint of Capstone Press
Mankato, Minnesota

Bridgestone Books are published by Capstone Press
151 Good Counsel Drive, P.O. Box 669, Mankato, Minnesota 56002
http://www.capstone-press.com

Library of Congress Cataloging-in-Publication Data
Feeney, Kathy, 1954–
    Sleep well: why you need to rest/by Kathy Feeney.
    p. cm.—(Your health)
    Includes bibliographical references and index.
    ISBN 0-7368-0970-8 (hardcover)
    ISBN 0-7368-4452-X (paperback)
    1. Sleep—Juvenile literature. [1. Sleep.] [DNLM: 1. Sleep—Juvenile literature. WL 108
F295s 2002] I. Title. II. Series.
RA786 .F44 2002
612.8′21—dc21   00-012534

Summary: An introduction to the benefits of sleep, including a discussion on dreaming,
    nightmares, sleepwalking, insomnia, and tips on how to sleep well.

Editorial Credits
Sarah Lynn Schuette, editor; Karen Risch, product planning editor; Linda Clavel,
    designer and illustrator

Photo Credits
Capstone Press/Gary Sundermeyer, 1, 8 (inset), 10, 12
Comstock, Inc., 16
Gregg R. Andersen, cover, 6, 14, 18, 20
PhotoDisc, Inc., 4

**Bridgestone Books thanks Mari Schuh and Rebecca Glaser, Mankato, Minnesota for providing
photo shoot locations.**

1 2 3 4 5 6 07 06 05 04 03 02

Table of Contents

You Need Sleep

Getting a good night's sleep is important. You do not have enough energy when you are tired. You may not be able to think clearly. Sleep helps your body rest and relax.

energy
the strength to do things without getting tired

5

Guess What?

Yawning seems to be contagious or catching. Did you yawn when you read this sentence?

How Much Sleep Do You Need?

Yawning usually is a sign that you are tired. Everyone needs different amounts of sleep. You usually need 9 to 10 hours of sleep to feel rested.

yawn
to open your mouth wide
and breathe in deeply

The Sleep Cycle

Awake

Stage 1

Falling Asleep
This stage lasts 1 to 7 minutes.

Stage 2

Light Sleep
You spend half of the
sleep cycle in this stage.

REM

Rapid Eye Movement
Dreaming and nightmares
happen during this stage.

Stages 3 and 4

Deep and Quiet Sleep
Sleepwalking happens
during these stages.

The Sleep Cycle

Your brain sends messages to parts of your body when you sleep. These messages tell your body to relax. Your body goes through the sleep cycle several times during the night.

sleep cycle

stages of sleep; changes in brain waves cause these stages.

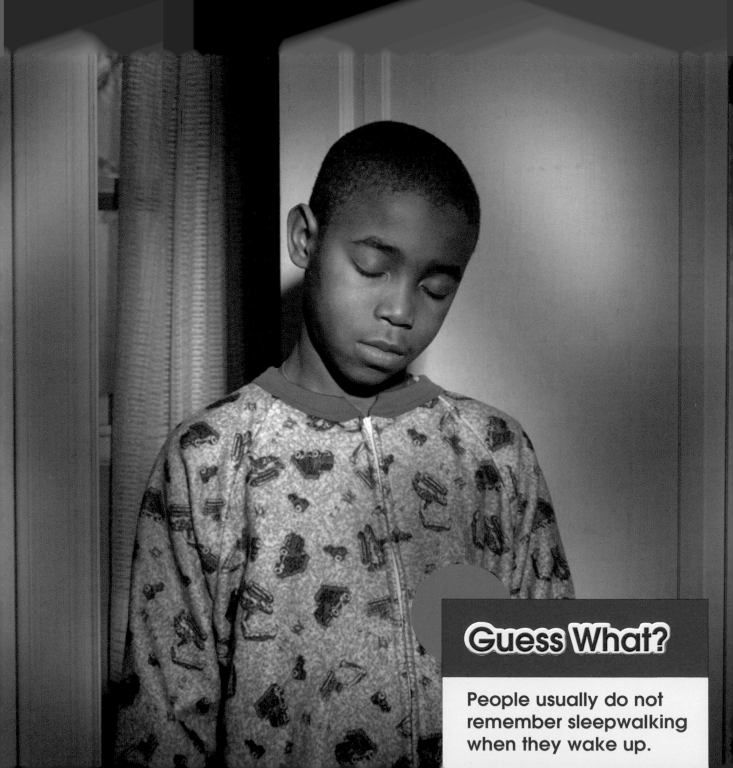

Guess What?

People usually do not remember sleepwalking when they wake up.

Sleepwalking

Some people walk during their deep sleep stage. They get up and walk around without waking up. People sometimes sleepwalk with their eyes closed. Other people look like they are awake.

Guess What?

Most people change their sleeping position more than 30 times in one night. This action often is called "tossing and turning."

Talking in Your Sleep

Many people talk in their sleep. They often sound like they are talking to another person. People who talk in their sleep seem to be awake. You usually do not remember talking in your sleep. You can talk in your sleep during each stage of the sleep cycle.

Dreaming

The last stage of the sleep cycle is called Rapid Eye Movement, or REM. Your eyelids are closed during REM. But your eyes move back and forth. You dream during this part of the sleep cycle.

Try This!

Talk about your nightmares with someone you trust. Remember that nightmares are not real.

Nightmares

A nightmare is a bad dream. You may feel scared, angry, or sad when you have a nightmare. You sometimes wake up during nightmares. Nightmares also happen during REM.

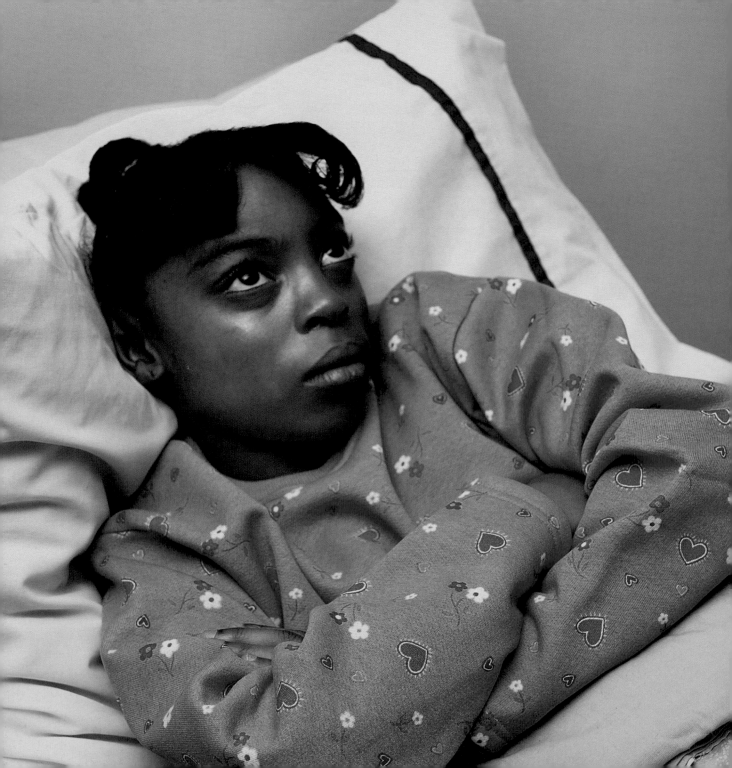

When You Cannot Sleep

You sometimes may have trouble falling asleep. You may be nervous about a test at school. You cannot relax or fall asleep. Some people have insomnia. They do not get the sleep they need. Doctors usually can help people with insomnia.

insomnia
not being able to fall asleep or stay asleep

Sleeping Well

Going to bed at the same time each night helps you sleep well. Waking up at the same time each morning helps your body follow a schedule. You will feel rested and ready for each day when you sleep well.

schedule
a plan for doing a task or a job

21

Hands On: Keep a Dream Diary

Scientists think people dream four or five times each night. Most people do not remember their dreams. The best way to remember your dreams is to write them down.

What You Need

Notebook
Pencil
Flashlight

What You Do

1. Keep the notebook and pencil next to your bed.
2. When you wake up in the morning, stay in bed for a few minutes to think about your dreams.
3. Write down everything you remember from your dreams.
4. Keep a flashlight next to your bed in case you wake up in the middle of the night. The flashlight will help you see in the dark when you write in your diary.
5. Read your dream diary each week. Are there any dreams that you had more than once?

Words to Know

energy (EN-ur-jee)—the strength to do things without getting tired; the right amount of sleep gives people energy.

insomnia (in-SOM-nee-uh)—not being able to fall asleep or stay asleep; some people who have insomnia wake up many times during the night.

nightmare (NITE-mair)—a bad dream; people sometimes feel scared during and after a nightmare.

schedule (SKED-jool)—a plan for doing a task or a job; following a sleep schedule helps the body feel rested.

Read More

Kent, Susan. *Let's Talk about When You Have Trouble Going to Sleep.* The Let's Talk Library. New York: PowerKids Press, 2000.

McPhee, Andrew T. *Sleep and Dreams.* New York: Franklin Watts, 2001.

Internet Sites

Brain POP: Sleep Movie
http://www.brainpop.com/health/nervous/sleep/index.weml
What Is Sleep and Why Do We Do It?
http://faculty.washington.edu/chudler/sleep.html
Why Do I Yawn?
http://kidshealth.org/kid/talk/qa/yawn.html

Index